This Coloring Book Belongs To

____

EASILY
DISTRACTED
BY
SNOW MONKEYS

Feeling
GOOD
Like
I Should

I JUST
FREAKING
Love
MONKEYS,
OK

POSITIVE
VIBES

MONKEYS
MAKE ME
HAPPY
YOU, NOT SO MUCH

Just be Cool!

NOTHIN'
BUTT
MONKEYS

FOLLOW
YOUR
DREAM

SNOW
MONKEY
WHISPERER

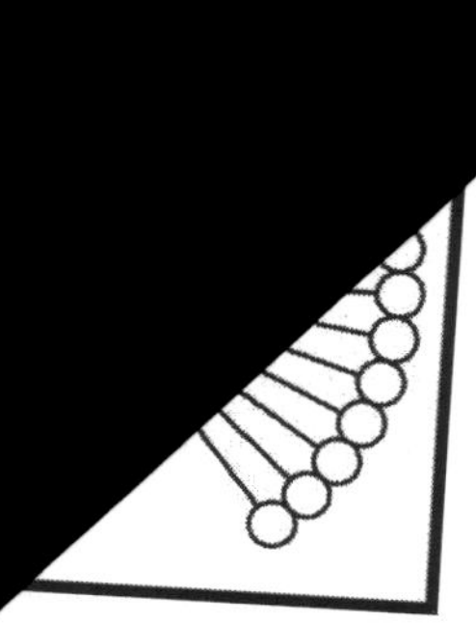

WANNA
HANG OUT?

Made in United States
Troutdale, OR
07/22/2023

11471116R00024